The Khmer Empire: The History and Legacy of One of Southeast Asia's Most Influential Empires

By Charles River Editors

Angkor Wat

## About Charles River Editors

**Charles River Editors** is a boutique digital publishing company, specializing in bringing history back to life with educational and engaging books on a wide range of topics. Keep up to date with our new and free offerings with this 5 2nd sign up on our weekly mailing list, and visit Our Kindle Author Page to see other recently published Kindle titles.

We make these books for you and always want to know our readers' opinions, so we encourage you to leave reviews and look forward to publishing new and exciting titles each week.

# Introduction

**Angkor Wat**

## The Khmer Empire

The Khmer Empire, also known as the Angkor Empire, was a powerful empire of Southeast Asia that was established in 802 CE and ended in 1431 with the invasion of the Siamese and abandonment of Angkor. The Khmer Empire was responsible for many of the historic monuments and temples found throughout the jungles of modern-day Cambodia, and also in other countries of Southeast Asia, all made possible by the fact the Khmer Empire reached across modern-day Cambodia, parts of Thailand, Laos, and Vietnam, making it a strategic trading partner with ships traveling from China and India.

Of all the architecture, the empire is best known for constructing Angkor Wat, one of the modern world's greatest wonders. Known in English as Angkor Wat ("City Temple"), the gigantic complex was built by King Suryavarman II in the early 12th century to serve as the king's state temple and capital city. Since it has remained so finely preserved, it has maintained religious significance for nearly 900 years, first dedicated to the Hindu god Vishnu, and then Buddhist. Understandably, it has become one of Cambodia's most potent symbols and tourist attractions, and it even appears on the Cambodian national flag. Angkor Wat continues to fascinate the world, both due to its sheer grandeur and size, as well as its ornamental decorations both inside and out. With political strife in Cambodia having cooled, Angkor Wat is now a major tourist attraction, bringing upwards of over half a million foreigners per year, which accounts for over half of the nation's tourists.

As a result, the long-lasting influence that this empire had on the people of Cambodia can still be felt today, with Angkor Wat being featured on the national flag. *The Khmer Empire: The History and Legacy of One of Southeast Asia's Most Influential Empires* chronicles the remarkable history of the Khmer and their impact on the region. Along with pictures depicting important people, places, and events, you will learn about the Khmer Empire like never before.

## The Region

The Khmer Empire is best known for its large monuments, and other ancient sites from this empire still dot Cambodia's landscape due in large measure to the character of the land itself. For example, one common relic of the empire is the use of reservoirs, which remains an essential part of everyday life in Cambodia. The importance of these reservoirs largely has to do with Cambodia's geography, as it is dominantly a giant, flat plain with low mountain ranges (Cardamom Hills to the west and the Dangrek Mountains to the east). Running from north to south is the Mekong River, which flows slightly westward through Phnom Penh, Cambodia's modern-day capital. From there, it continues south toward Vietnam and branches out across the flat plains into numerous smaller streams, and from there it runs into the South China Sea. This river is roughly 4,200 kilometers long and is the fourth largest river (in terms of volume of flow) in Asia, beginning in Tibet (Zéphir 1998: 15). The Kulen Mountain region is near Angkor, considered the ancient capital of the Khmer Empire, but for the most part, the landscape is flat with the occasional hill, known as *phnoms*. These would play a significant role in the Khmer Empire's history, as they helped determine where rulers would establish their mortuary temples. The ancient belief in sacred hills is still alive today since almost every *phnom* is capped with a sacred Buddhist pagoda. These modern religious sites tend to be built on or very near ancient Khmer sites that were mostly dedicated to Hindu gods.

Cambodia's climate is affected by monsoons that result in dry and wet seasons. From around November-May, the climate is generally dry with high temperatures, which makes life difficult, especially from March-April. It is this seasonal drought period that made the construction of reservoirs a priority for any ruler, and this dependence on the water contributed to the development of sacred beliefs and mythology surrounding the water. If the seasonal cycle continues, the rainy season begins around June and lasts through October. These periods bring particularly heavy rain during the end of the season.

The heavy rainfall during the wet season has an enormous effect on the great lake known as Tonlé Sap, located in the middle of the vast plains. From June on, the lake rises, resulting in it almost quadrupling in size by the end of the rainy season. The monsoons are so powerful and the flow of the water is so strong that the Tonlé Sap River, flowing from Tonlé Sap to Phnom Penh and the Mekong, actually reverses its flow for a time due to the excessive flow of water. It also provides an ideal breeding ground for freshwater fish. The Tonlé Sap is, in fact, one of the largest sources of freshwater fish in Southeast Asia, even today, and it is likely that these waters played a significant role in the establishment of Angkor on the northern bank, just beyond the reach of high flood waters.

Fresh water is necessary for human survival in any part of the world, not only for quenching thirst but as a source of food and irrigation. Such a dependence on water and the dangerous droughts during the dry season led to the development of supernatural beliefs surrounding the life-giving waters. In the days before the Khmer Empire, the waters were symbolized by a mythical snake known as a *naga*, a multi-headed cobra associated with water and the benefits it provided, such as wealth through abundant crops.

The founding of Cambodia is even associated with a mythical serpent. The myth states that a Brahman of India named Kaundinya married the local snake-princess, named Soma. From this marriage, the first ancient royal lineage of Cambodia, the monarchs of Funan, a predecessor state to the Khmer Empire, was formed. It is possible this symbolic meeting between a foreign Indian priest and a local "snake" princess is based in some truth, such as the marriage of a foreign Indian priest or royalty to a local princess of people associated with sacred waters. The influence of Indian civilization on local populations, as will be discussed below, had a significant effect on the development of early civilizations of Cambodia and the Khmer.

Before the first civilizations had developed, beginning in the 1st or 2nd century CE, the people who entered Southeast Asia likely followed sources of freshwater from the north to the south. This much is linguistically supported by philologists linking the pre-Khmer people to the Yangzi Valley near Tibet. By 500 BCE, the pre-civilization inhabitants had become skilled bronze-workers and iron-workers. One tradition coming with these early inhabitants was the cultivation of rice. Once the monsoonal seasons were understood and local farmers were able to develop irrigation systems for farming rice, population sizes grew with the surplus of food. Larger populations that grew beyond extended families typically required an authority figure to maintain control through the establishment of rules or laws.

Since there are virtually no written records of or by the people during this period, it is difficult to understand what or how this authoritative rule may have been practiced. If the mythological founding of Funan has any truth behind it, it is possible that local city-states were ruled by regional royal families. What is understood of this time is that civilizations did not begin to develop until trade with India became commonplace and local rulers took advantage of city-states located near beneficial, navigational waters. Local ruling powers had control over what could be deemed large regions, but they were generally ruled from a fortified city.

The political network created through interaction between ruling powers formed a unique political structure, known as a *mandala* (Higham 1991). The name of this unique ruling structure comes from India and may refer to a magical, sacred diagram used in tantric rituals. In general, the circular mandala is meant to represent the universe and is frequently represented in paintings and dances such as the *mandala-nrtya,* symbolizing the constant presence of the gods (Cotterell and Storm 2009: 341). In a political context, the mandala refers to a local ruler's relationship with his territory, which is generally viewed as a circle, much like the tantric diagram. The power of the mandala and its central point could always change with variables such as invasion, trade influences, or whoever had political power within the mandala (Higham 1991: 240). The center of the mandala could also shift from one city center to another when a new king or prince took power, or it could be absorbed when a local prince swore loyalty to a more powerful ruler.

## Funan

By the 2nd century CE, India had firmly established trade contacts with Southeast Asia. The visitors from India were not interested in establishing colonies in Southeast Asia, but in obtaining the wealth they believed located there. Nonetheless, the pre-Khmer people were influenced to adopt numerous Indian traditions, in a process known as Indianization, which would result in numerous ideas and traditions becoming part of Khmer culture (Deedrick 2002). As more and more Indians established trading routes in and through Cambodia (to reach China), it is possible that traders and locals found it more beneficial to adopt the customs of these foreign traders. While the traders likely spread their beliefs to the willing locals, priests and gurus from India also traveled to Cambodia where they could teach Indian religions, scripts, and laws. It was through this contact that the holy script—known as Sanskrit—was adopted. Sanskrit's influence would have a lasting effect on local rulers and would be used by the Khmer rulers much later for inscriptions on monuments and buildings.

No architecture or inscriptions from this early period have survived, suggesting the early structures had been made from perishable, organic materials, such as wood, which does not preserve well in such damp climates. There are, however, historical records available from the time, since visiting traders from India and China had developed writing. It is from these foreign accounts that historians have the name of Funan, although it is uncertain if the people used the term to refer to themselves.

The first reports of the Funan came to European knowledge from the works of Paul Pelliot in 1903 when he began translating 3rd century CE Chinese reports of maritime trade, recorded by Kang Dai and Zhu Ying, envoys of the Wu emperor. According to his translations of the Dai and Ying texts, there were walled settlements and palaces for various rulers who had enacted a system of taxation to collect gold, silver, perfumes, and pearls. The kingdom itself is described as "more than 3000 li [one li equals 540 meters] west of Linyi [also known as Champa situated in central and southern Vietnam] in a large bay of the sea…There are walled towns, palaces and dwelling houses. The men…practice farming…They like to engrave ornaments and to carve…They have books and keep archives…The characters of their writing resemble those of the Hou [a people from central Asia with writing developed from Indian characters]." (Higham 2013: 101-102).

The Funan had also developed specialized metal workers and engravers. The commoners lived in modest houses on small raised hills that helped protect them from the regular floods taking place. A representative of the Indian Murunda king was noted as having a residence established in the mandala. According to Dai and Ying, this alliance between the Funan and the Murunda king may have been the result of a marriage between an Indian named Kaundinya and a local princess.

There is very little known about the rulers of Funan, although some of the rulers are mentioned in Dai and Ying. In the Chinese accounts, rulers are often given the title of *pan* or *fan*, which may have been a Chinese version of the Khmer title, *pon,* that would be used later. A small collection of local inscriptions from the 5th century CE detail an increasing pressure or conflict from India, resulting in the local rulers adopting certain Indian customs, the most notable of which is the addition of the Sanskrit language and Indian royal titles. An example of the adoption of a new Indian title can be found in an inscription fragment detailing a name beginning with *Ja-*. This may have been in reference to Jayavarman of Funan (c. 480 CE), whose name included the term *varman,* meaning "shield" in Sanskrit. Further evidence of this Indian influence comes from the construction ordered by Jayavarman of Funan, who ordered numerous Hindu temples devoted to foreign gods built, especially the god Vishnu.

Vishnu is often seen as one of the most important Hindu deities, but he is one of a triad of major gods. Along with Shiva and Brahma, they form what is known as the *Trimurti*. The role of Vishnu is often-changing as are his many avatars, but it was to act as preserver of the world. Devotees to Vishnu—like Jayavarman of Funan—are known as *Vaishnavas,* and they revere him as the supreme god to the point where Vishnu is depicted in place of the god Brahma, a Hindu god viewed as the absolute or supreme reality (Cotterell and Storm 2009: 356-357). For a ruler, Vishnu is seen as the logical choice for devotion, since the god is seen as the ultimate representation of good over evil. The influence Vishnu had on pre-Khmer and Khmer rulers is found on surviving monuments and inscriptions, although they may not refer to Vishnu directly. For instance, Vishnu assumes numerous forms throughout the Indian sagas, such as Rama in the epic poem, the *Ramayana*. Since these representations play an integral part in the beliefs and works of art created by Khmer rulers and people, it is worth taking a moment to review some of Vishnu's avatars and deeds.

Avatars assumed by Vishnu were a part of the deep involvement and attachment the god was believed to have with mankind. During times of hardship or when the world was threatened by evil, it was believed the god would descend to earth in a process that has taken place roughly ten times. In Vishnu's first incarnation, he became a fish known as Matsya, who rescued a man named Manu from being eaten by a larger fish. He then warned Manu of an impending flood and helped him build a boat to save animals and seeds with which to repopulate the world. The second avatar is that of Kurma, the tortoise, who helped assist with the churning of the ocean of milk, in a scene famously depicted in the galleries of Angkor Wat. The third avatar was as Varsha, the boar, rescuer of earth from the demon Hiranyaksha. The fourth incarnation was as Narasimha, a man-lion who disemboweled the demon Hiranyakashipu. Vishnu's fifth incarnation was as a mythical dwarf who rescued the earth from the demon Bali. His sixth avatar differs from the other animal-like forms. This time, Vishnu became Parashurama, a man borne of the

Brahman—or priest—caste, destined to become the warrior who wielded a mythical axe from Shiva. In revenge for an insult to his father, Parashurama killed all males of the warrior caste and made the widows sleep with the males of the Brahman caste to create a new, purer, warrior caste.

Continuing the tradition of human avatars, Vishnu's seventh avatar is perhaps one of the most famous. Here, Vishnu takes the form of Rama—the son of King Ayodhya—in a quest to destroy the demon Ravana. After killing Ravana and rescuing his wife, he ruled for a thousand years. Like the churning of the ocean of milk, this scene is also depicted in the galleries at Angkor Wat. Vishnu's eighth incarnation is as Krishna, who destroyed many demons and assisted the hero Arjuna. The ninth incarnation—also one popular in Khmer culture—was as Gautama Buddha. The identification of this avatar did not come about until around the 4th century CE, which may help explain the willingness and acceptance of Buddhism in Southeast Asia. The 10th and supposedly final version of Vishnu, Kalkin, is said to have arrived at the end of the current age, known as the *Kali Yuga* (Cotterell and Storm 2009: 338-417).

It may have been during Jayavarman of Funan's rule that Sanskrit was incorporated into the everyday life of the elites. From the limited texts and descriptions of the way of life during this time, it seems there was still frequent feuding between local powers with the ruler, Citrasena's, eventual conquering of Funan, shifting the mandala's central power to Chenla (alternatively written Zhenla, Tchen-La or Kambuja) (Maurice 1944).

The Funan—and later Khmer—economic systems were dependent on the surplus of rice production. This valuable agricultural product was required to sustain the mandala, the specialization of metalworking, and trade. Chinese visitors note rice production, but the exact methods used during the Funan period are not known. To control production and distribution, it is certain that a strong administrative system had to have been in place, yet despite the need for central administration, it is difficult to determine whether the Funan—as described by the Chinese—regarded themselves as a single, unified state. Even though archaeological evidence shows a series of canals connecting large walled settlements—such as Oc Eo in southern Vietnam with Angkor Borei (Higham 1991)—this, in itself, does not mean there was a single, political power ruling at the time, but rather, multiple rulers competing for power. One way these smaller powers would have competed with each other was through influencing trade.

The extent of trade can be found in the archaeological evidence with artifacts from as far away as Rome having been uncovered in Oc Eo. This transcontinental trade extended over China and India to the Roman Empire, forming the Silk Road. Since the Funan mandala was located on the delta of the Mekong River, it was ideally placed for controlling shipping access to China. This, on the one hand, made the rulers of these regions wealthy and prosperous, but an over-dependence on trade with external powers left them vulnerable to changes taking place overseas. For the Funan rulers, the decision of the Chinese to bypass the delta region to establish trade routes directly with Java proved particularly disastrous. In addition, frequent struggles with other local rulers caused the mandala's political center to shift from the former trade center of the delta to the mainland (Higham 2004:113), leading to the eventual abandonment of Oc Eo and Angkor Borei sometime between the fifth and seventh centuries.

## Chenla

Long after the collapse of the Funan and Chenla, 10th century inscriptions tell the legend of the founding of the Chenla kingdom. Like the Indian-influenced legend of Funan founding, so, too, are elements of Indian influence present in Chenla legend, which says Shiva himself bestowed the hand of celestial nymph Nera in marriage to hermit Kambu Svayambhuva. Kambu—whose name suggests he is the eponymous ancestor of Cambodia—and Mera produced a royal lineage of kings to which future rulers of the Khmer Empire would claim lineage. Since this legend was established in the 10th century, it is highly likely that elements of the story were integrated and/or changed to suit the needs of rulers, such as which kings were Kambu and Mera's actual ancestors. It is also worth noting that the origin of the term, Khmer, may have also developed from this legend through the combination of the names Kambu and Mera (Zéphir 1998: 26-27).

10th century legends aside, the mandala's central power shifted mainland between the fifth and seventh centuries, as did the merchant traders and chronicles of their travels (Vickery 1998). Like the textual information available for Funan, some of the best historical sources for Chenla come from Chinese travelers. A compilation of Chinese texts in the 13th century by Ma Duanlin contains a description of an early 7th century ruler who was, most likely, King Ishanavarman, who was said to have given audiences every three days in extravagant halls in which he would adorn himself with a gold crown decorated with valuable stones. Visitors of the court were said to have bowed their heads to the ground three times, and at the end of the audience, members of the court prostrated themselves. These texts reveal a complex social hierarchy heavily involved in the display of wealth and power. Furthermore, the Chinese accounts detail some of the struggles taking place during the decline of the Funan polity, as lands in the interior had begun to make themselves more independent (the largest inland state being Chenla).

It should be considered that Ma Dualin's accounts of Ma Dualin were compiled in the 13th century, and that 7th century events may have been obscured over time. The archaeology of the Chenla period in the region, particularly of temple inscriptions which survive much longer than text written on organic materials, suggests there was no centrally unified Chenla authority (Higham 1991). In other words, there is no primary source of information indicating a single, unified Chenla power. There may, instead, have been a powerful mandala that exerted control over other local powers. Whether the people identified themselves as part of a central Chenla authority is uncertain. This may be the result of the limits of the archaeological evidence, since the inscriptions that have survived (mainly those inscribed on temples) may have served specific functions, such as listing benefactors or dedications, which would not require the mention of a central Chenla authority or the view of the commoners. More often than not, the ways and customs of the common people are not mentioned at all, except where the issue of taxation and its collection are mentioned (which commonly took place in the temples).

There is some historical evidence contradicting Ma Dualin's account of struggles during the transition of power. Inscriptions from the Chenla brick temple Kdei Ang, established in 667 CE, lists the names of an elite family, beginning with King Rudravarman of Funan (514-550). The inscription goes on to list the maternal nephews (Dharmadeva and Simhadeva) who served Kings Bhavavarman I and Mahendravarman; Simhavira, a maternal nephew of Dharmadeva, who served under King Ishanavarman; and Simhadatta, who served King Jayavarman I (of Chenla). King Ishanavarman also took a wife from this lineage (Higham 2001: 38). Inscriptions such as this, bridging to political transition from Funan to Chenla, suggest a relatively smooth transition. Nonetheless, still little is known of how these rulers effectively functioned. It is possible these increasingly important social hierarchies are the result of Indian influences—for example, the emphasis placed on matrilineal descent. Other influences becoming more evident were the increased use of Sanskrit for personal and place names, as well as unique architectural styles.

The construction of monuments and temples dedicated to kings or rulers is perhaps an idea borrowed from India, where numerous stelae helped solidify a king's rule and enforce his laws. Alternatively, this could have been an idea arising independently, since it is a phenomenon found in ancient Egypt and pre-Columbian cultures of Mesoamerica and South America (Ricci 2014). The similarity in architecture from the Chenla and later powers to that of contemporary India suggests this projection of power through building was a borrowed idea. The monuments constructed would serve a multitude of functional and ceremonial purposes. Already mentioned above is the fact that taxes were collected in temples. Temple inscriptions frequently mention boundaries of rice fields often bordering forests, roads, and reservoirs. They also list temple personnel, such as priests, musicians, dancers, and craft specialists (e.g., leaf sewers, potters, weavers, and spinners). The temples were also utilized as meeting points for exchanging goods and ideas during ceremonial gatherings. Ceremonies at monumental constructions acted as opportunities for local communities to interact with other, distant communities with whom they would otherwise have little to no contact. This allowed for trade and more importantly, the forming of long-term relationships through marriage arrangements.

Based on inscriptions from temples, it is assumed Chenla's economic system was more or less agrarian in nature and revolved around the temples, which also served as a way for the king or overlord to make their power known to the people. Since literacy was not entirely common among lower-class farmers, images displaying the might and power of authority were frequently used in a practice maintained and elaborated upon in the later, Khmer Empire. One example from the Chenla era comes from a lintel at Wat En Khna displaying the king on his throne along with members of the royal court. Accompanying the image are inscriptions offering details regarding the individuals, such as their names, titles, duties, and details of their economic duties.

From these inscriptions, it is known the temples were also places to manage agricultural surpluses.

These functions are detailed in temple inscriptions that go over the provisions required for personnel, while elite individuals are mentioned for their roles in temple management. These elite, *pon*-titled individuals—*pon* was an inherited title, while other royal names combined the Sanskrit words *jaya* or *mahendra* with titles that were not inherited—could donate their communal land and organize their kin to produce surpluses for the temple. It should be noted that although gold, silver, and precious stones were traded at this time, wealth was primarily accumulated in the form of rice, cloth, and land (Higham 1996). When an individual accumulated a significant amount of wealth within the temple which housed the ancestral spirits, it was believed the person would have a more prosperous reincarnation. The *pon* could then trade cloth and rice for gold and silver, while the land could be mortgaged to the temple with the produce from the land acting as a form of interest payment. Individuals could essentially continue collecting wealth until they were able to buy more land or accumulate it through marriage until they controlled a significant amount. Such actions would necessarily be watched very closely by the king since this might have led to the establishment of future rivals.

Inscriptions and images on temples indicate that by the early 7th century, royal centers and rural lands acknowledged a hereditary ranking system. It is from this developing system that the kings obtained their political power and maintained it by employing local rulers and members of the court to operate on his behalf. Local leaders were in charge of developing and constructing new temples for ancestral spirits; since the *pon* often claimed descent from these high-ranking, ancestral spirits, it was important they enforce offerings to these temples. The temples themselves were narrow, tall, and corbel-vaulted, located on a raised platform, commonly enclosed in a square or rectangular enclosure, and made from brick, although stone and wood were sometimes incorporated. The entrance featured a sandstone lintel with carvings, while the interior featured the state *linga* (discussed below) and various statues.

Large, religious complexes were also developed at this time, including sites such as Sambor Prei Kuk by Ishanavarman I. According to inscriptions at this site (specifically the southern section of the site, featuring three temples), he had established control over the majority of Cambodia, although how this control or rule functioned is unknown. Some of the earliest, non-imported, religious icons are found from this period, the earliest of which dates back to the 5th or 6th century. Hinduism and Buddhism developed side-by-side in Southeast Asia during this time. As indicated by the founding myths of Funan and Chenla, the religions evolved independently of India by incorporating local mythologies or beliefs into the imported Hindu and Buddhist beliefs.

Temples were central meeting places for trade, rule, and worship. The importance of Vishnu in the Funan era has already been touched upon, but Hinduism and Buddhism as a whole must be understood to know how the temples functioned as areas of worship. Buddhism, in general, follows the teachings of the Buddha. Before achieving enlightenment, Buddha lived a series of lives as a *bodhisattva,* an enlightened being destined to become a Buddha—the *bodhisattva* puts off the moment of entering nirvana, thereby escaping the cycle of death and rebirth to teach people the path toward enlightenment. The Buddha was eventually born as Siddhartha Gautama to King Suddhodana. When Siddhartha Gautama was 12 years old, the king was told a prophecy that for his son to be king, he must not witness the miseries of life. To prevent his son from witnessing any suffering, Siddhartha grew up isolated in the palace and was prevented from looking outside. He eventually married Yasodhara who bore him a son, Rahula, but by age 30, he had wandered out of his palace of isolation to witness four "sights": old age, disease, death, and a person looking to transcend suffering. He tried to do the same by denying himself much of life for the next six years. This did not bring him closer to enlightenment, so he set off for Bodh Gaya, where he sat beneath a bodhi tree (in some versions it is a banyan tree). It was there he was tempted by the demon Mara, and he became aware of the Four Noble Truths: life is suffering; suffering depends on conditions like craving; these conditions can be removed; and to remove the suffering, one must follow the eightfold path, requiring one to practice right: view, thought, speech, action, livelihood, effort, mindfulness, and contemplation. At that moment, he became Gautama Buddha, the founder of Buddhism, and he preached for more than 40 years before achieving nirvana at 80 years of age (Cotterell and Storm 2009: 368-372).

Along with Buddhism, Hinduism was also practiced. Shiva and Vishnu are the gods that had a significant influence on the Khmer Empire and pre-Khmer rulers. Vishnu and his avatars have already been discussed as a favored deity, but Shiva, at times, was also popular. In contrast to Vishnu, the protector of the world, was Shiva, the destroyer, a part of the Trimurti and considered god of creation, time (hence, destruction), and fertility. The focus of Shiva as a symbol of fertility may have been an important aspect for ruling powers who wished to pass their rule to their kin. Shiva is often represented as a *lingam* or *linga,* which is a phallic-shaped stone. According to Hindu mythology, Shiva had visited a pine forest where sages were deep in meditation. The sages did not recognize the god and accused him of trying to seduce their wives. So enraged were the sages that they swiftly cut off the phallus of the god, causing the world to grow dark and the virility of the sages to disappear. It was only after countless offerings to Shiva that balance to the world was restored. This seemingly obscure myth would become a central reason for the construction of temples, which would house monumental sacred *lingam* that rulers would name after themselves. It is also this strong connection with the lingam that early historians believed the focal center of Chenla to be at Mount Phu Kao, also known as *Lingaparvata,* meaning the mountain of the *linga.* Shiva is, nevertheless, able to take a number of different forms but is commonly represented with four arms and a necklace of skulls around his neck. Statues or representations of him and events of his life are commonly found in monuments and temples.

As far as notable rulers of Chenla, the great-grandson of Ishanavarman, Jayavarman I of Chenla, was the one who may have brought smaller mandalas together, thereby establishing a number of vassal kings (Higham 1996: 370). He exerted considerable control over a wide region, based on inscriptions found in the lowlands bordering the Mekong River, through the Great Lake in the north, and west to the agricultural region of Battambang. He was also responsible for the creation of new titles and administrators. The capital of Jayavarman I of Chenla was known as Purandarapura, but archaeologists have yet to discover the exact location of this site. He also expanded the army as a means to defend his land, but also for the absorption of nearby territories through conquest. Jayavarman I of Chenla was also responsible for developing and enforcing a legal code for his land, though little else is known about other ruling dynasties and Chenla's smaller states. What is known is that one kingdom was centered on Stung Treng and followed the Mekong to as far north as the Mun River. This kingdom likely based its wealth on controlling river trade. Another kingdom was known as Canasapura and was located in the upper Mun area (Higham 2004).

Inscriptions and archaeological evidence suggest that during this period of early state formation there were numerous competing polities. Inscriptions from Jayavarman I of Chenla are found over a wide region of the Mekong Delta, along the river, and surrounding the Tonlé Sap. These inscriptions bear the name of authorities appointed by Jayavarman I of Chenla, indicating a tightening of control over the region. This was the beginning of a new administrative rule for the lands. Through this administration, Jayavarman I of Chenla could collect taxes and control the distribution and use of the land. Other inscriptions hint at the level of conflict still present during state formation (that is to say they do not directly list battles, conflicts, or victories). For example, it is stated that innumerable vassal kings obeyed his command, and while in combat, he was considered the living incarnation of victory, the scourge of his enemies, and the conqueror of more lands (Higham 2004: 167).

While the higher frequency of these inscriptions detailing both the deeds of rulers and the collection of taxes can be an indication of a more or less stable kingdom, fewer inscriptions typically indicate severe conflict or instability within the kingdom. The number of inscriptions of the Chenla mandala declines sometime around the 8th century. The mandala had become separated into lower coastal and upper inland Chenlas, if, indeed, the people had ever viewed themselves as a single, united one. The location of the lower coastal Chenla made it a prosperous location for trade given its proximity to the sea, but it also made the mandala an easy target for hostile, foreign naval forces. During this period, the Malayan Empire, known as Srivijaya, had assumed control of Java and Sumatra and proceeded to attack the lower coastal Chenla. During this period, the historical record essentially goes dark, and details of rule are difficult to establish.

The presence of raiding and conquering foreign powers from Java is significant during this period since it is recorded that Jayavarman II (reigned 770-834 CE), founder of the Khmer Empire, grew up in the midst of these conflicts. One of the few, surviving inscriptions from this dark period comes from Sdok Kak Thom and details how one of Java's rulers took Jayavarman II. Some scholars doubt the authenticity of the accounts claiming Jayavarman II was taken to the

Indonesian island of Java for a time (Vickery 1998), arguing it is more likely Jayavarman II was brought to the neighboring Cham Empire. During this period, there were also frequent conflicts with the Chams, and Jayavarman II began his career in politics in eastern Cambodia, near the Cham Empire. It has also been argued that Jayavarman II's early architecture shows both Cham and Javanese influences, allowing for an alternative possibility. Whatever the case, it is possible that during his time away, Jayavarman II encountered a ruler assuming a god-like role of authority and who reigned over sacred courts. Little is actually known of what happened to Jayavarman II during this time, but his actions upon returning to Cambodia in 770 suggest he had been influenced by his trip or time away.

Upon his return to Cambodia, Jayavarman II began to compete with and conquer mandalas such as Śambhupura, Aninditapura, and Prithivīnarendra. Tactics employed by Jayavarman II were not always violent. In fact, a number of local princes were actually drawn to his charismatic leadership (Higham 2004). Incentives that would have been offered to such local princes included tracts of land that had either been taken from conquered rival territories or those destined to be conquered. A high rank within Jayavarman II's court would have also been a valuable incentive, giving local princes the chance to be a part of the politics of the newly forming kingdom. It also offered the future possibility of marrying into the royal family. Local royals would eagerly offer their daughters to be the wives of Jayavarman II or of any sons he had. After several decades of conquering and uniting smaller kingdoms into a larger one, Jayavarman II was ready to enact a ceremony no previous Cambodian ruler had carried out before, that would serve as a precedent for future kings for hundreds of years.

## The Establishment of the Khmer Empire

**A map of the region with the Khmer Empire in red**

Although Jayavarman II had come to power and was consolidating his power by 770, it was not complete until he had proclaimed himself *kamraten jagat ta raja,* or "the God who is king," also known as *devaraja.* He held a coronation to mark this event in 802, which is now recognized as the official beginning of the Khmer Empire. It is uncertain from where this concept had come, whether it was from his mysterious early days abroad in "Java," or if it was an independently developed idea. That said, the idea of establishing one's self as a divine ruler is found throughout the world, and it is, therefore, not entirely impossible Jayavarman II developed the idea without influence (Ricci 2014). The ceremony enacted in 802, however, was highly influenced by Hindu concepts and *Brāhmanic* rituals. It must be kept in mind, that the Hindu idea of a deity living on earth is not necessarily new. As mentioned above, Vishnu and Shiva have taken on numerous avatars on earth and so, having a king who was also a god was not too far-fetched for the people to accept.

By this time, Jayavarman II had already established himself as being linked with mythical founder Kambu Svayambhuva and celestial nymph Mera. This was known as the Aninditapura royal lineage mentioned in temple inscriptions tracing succession lineages. While kings typically had numerous children, inheritance of the throne was not necessarily based on a father-son relationship. Rather, the throne could be passed laterally, to a cousin or an uncle. Given that the rules governing the exchange of the throne were not clear, there was, at times, friction between family members that sometimes resulted in exile or small-scale war as parties competed for their perceived right to the throne.

Jayavarman II had already established Indrapura, a capital near Banteay Prei Nokor, but with Jayavarman II a devaraja, it was necessary for him to establish a new capital. Accordingly, the first of three capitals he would establish was at the site of his sacred-royal consecration; a site known as Mahendraparvata, meaning "Mountain of the Great Indra" in Sanskrit. The site had been chosen for its symbolic relationship within the Hindu religion. The concept of sacred hills or mountains is a factor featured throughout Khmer architecture and site planning. Although the idea of placing a capital on top of a mountain hill—one which had been a source of water for the Tonlé Sap—seemed like a good idea, it was impractical due to its remote location and inaccessibility.

This fascination with sacred mountains comes from India where the Himalayan Mountains inspired early Indians to make the peaks that no man could reach the place of the gods. Mount Meru was the central mountain around which the entire cosmos had been organized. In some myths, it is claimed that Indra himself is the creator of the great mountain. According to mythology, Indra had become displeased with a herd of flying elephants, and he cut off their wings, causing them to become the great mountain. This origin mythology may have been drawn upon by Jayavarman II when creating Mahendraparvata, the Mountain of the Great Indra, in an attempt to make a new Mount Meru. It would have been important for a devaraja to make himself a sacred mountain on earth, as it was believed that all spheres of existence—from the heavens to the netherworlds—focused around a sacred mountain. In India, it was also believed the sacred River Ganges flowed directly from Mount Meru, making it necessary to incorporate water systems, whether natural or artificial, into the construction of a sacred mountain on earth.

The other significant capital Jayavarman II founded was Hariharālaya, on the Tonlé Sap floodplain, making it easily accessible, yet out of reach from the waters during the wet season. The Tonlé Sap provided food and water to the people of the capital, while the river allowed access to the Mekong River. This, in turn, allowed the Khmer people to travel and trade with distant partners to the north and south while providing the Khmer with natural defenses. Due to the nature of the Mekong, with its naturally sandy banks and shifting currents, navigation of the river required an intimate knowledge of it that only the locals possessed. The size of the lake varies during the year, shrinking during the dry season (to only 2,700 square kilometers) and swelling during the wet season (to 10,000 square kilometers due to waters from melted snow and monsoonal rainfalls). These waters were so vital to the people they constructed floating houses able to rest on the land during the dry season and float during the wet season.

All that remains of this capital are a group of temples known as the Roluos Group, consisting of Preah Ko, the Bakong, and Lolei. It is unclear as to whether Jayavarman II had any part in the construction of these temples, but the capital name is a sign of its dedication to both Shiva and Vishnu. The first part of the capital's name, *Hari,* is in reference to one of Vishnu's many names, while *hara* is in reference to Hara, an alternative name for Shiva. This dual form of worship was not limited to names but also reflected in statues, depicting a half-Shiva, half-Vishnu god. The statues featured stylistic elements attributed to both of the gods. For example, the Shiva half held a *Trishula* (a form of trident) while the Vishnu half held a conch shell. This seems to be part of a tradition dating to the pre-Khmer period, as one recovered statue without arms but wearing a dual hairstyle and housed in the Metropolitan Museum of Art indicates (MMA 2017). On the left side of the statue is a crown-like object, which may be an actual crown, symbolic of Vishnu. The right side of the statue seemingly features hair—as indicated by an incised line, which may represent matted hair piled high—in a style which Shiva is known to wear as a yogic master.

It was in Hariharālaya that Jayavarman II died in 835. The succession of the throne passed on to Jayavarman II's son, Jayavarman III (reigned 835-877). There is very little known about this ruler except that only a few temples were built during his reign and he claimed to have built none of them. It is believed he may have died chasing a wild elephant after which succession of the throne passed to Indravarman I (reigned 877 to 889). Based on inscriptions, Indravarman I married Jayavarman II's granddaughter, although there are also inscriptions proclaiming Indravarman I was an invincible warrior who decimated enemies with his sword (Higham 2004: 149). Regardless of the content of the inscriptions, what can be understood of this ruler is that he was responsible for a number of constructions and architectural patterns at Hariharālaya. As mentioned above, the sacred-mountain-on-earth would also need to be associated with waters. Therefore, Indravarman I went about with the construction of a giant reservoir followed by a pyramid-temple meant to represent Mount Meru. Furthermore, since this was meant to be the center of the cosmic world where the gods lived, and the god-king would reign, it also needed to serve as his mausoleum.

The reservoir he began was beyond any basic reservoir the people would need to survive. It was meant to be the sacred waters of Mount Meru and therefore needed to be awe-inspiring for whoever visited his sacred temple-mount. The construction was unlike anything the people had seen before, measuring 3,800 by 800 meters, and according to inscriptions, was meant to reflect his glory like the ocean (Higham 2004: 149). One hundred and fifty times larger than any *baray* (reservoir) that had come before it and featuring advancements in construction techniques, he named it Indratataka, further linking his works with the gods as well as himself. Despite the size of the reservoir, there is no indication Indratataka was actually used to supply surrounding fields with water during droughts. What it did do was to assist in supplying moats of nearby temples with water. Two of these surviving temples from the Roluos Group are Preah Ko and the Bakong.

Preah Ko is a recent name applied to the temple meaning "sacred ox," due to the numerous statues of Siva's sacred mount, Nandi. The temple consists of three towers dedicated to Rudravarman and Prithivindravarman (the maternal grandfather and father of Indravarman I), while the central tower was dedicated to Jayavarman II. Temples such as these were meant to both honor the king's ancestors and act as large-scale visual credentials for the legitimacy of the king's rule (Zéphir 1998). This may have been especially important for Indravarman I, given his marriage into the royal line through the granddaughter of Jayavarman II, rather than through birth.

The other temple, the Bakong, served the dual role of being Indravarman I's mausoleum and the state shrine. This duality of a monument was followed (when possible) by the next thirteen Khmer kings. Just as the Indratataka was a massive construction project never seen before, so, too, was the Bakong. The exterior of the Bakong measured 800 by 650 meters and was a hundredfold greater in volume than anything built before it. The linga of the state, named Indresvara, was erected there in 881(Higham 1991: 325). The Bakong was also one of the earliest monuments to incorporate *nagas* into the architecture of bridges. Another notable construction design of the Bakong differing from previous rulers is the use of stone—rather than brick—in its construction. Such construction projects suggest there was a significant amount of control and organization during the rule of Indravarman I. The level of organization and the procurement of materials suggest the description of conflicts and Indravarman I as an invincible warrior may have been minor and did not upset the economic system of the empire.

Following the death of Indravarman I in 889, his son, Yaśovarman, took the throne, though the succession of the throne was not a peaceful one. Upon Indravarman I's death, a struggle ensued between Yaśovarman and his brother. It is believed that Indravarman I tried to block Yaśovarman's accession to the throne, which is why there are no shrines or monuments constructed by Yaśovarman honoring his father or Jayavarman II. Instead, he traced his ancestry through his mother back to Funan and Chenla kings (Briggs 1951).

As the new god-king on earth, it was his duty to establish a new sacred mountain on earth. Given the size of constructions left behind by his father and the fact the former state shrine was primarily acting as a mausoleum for his father, Yaśovarman relocated his court 15 kilometers to the northwest. It was there that a natural hill, known as the *Bakheng*, rose approximately 65 meters over the surrounding plains. Following the precedent set by his father, Yaśovarman began construction on Yasódharapura: his mausoleum and state temple. The state temple itself would only be consecrated shortly before Yaśovarman's death. Although he followed the construction pattern of his father, Yaśovarman went a step further to incorporate more symbolism in his projects. Yasódharapura was enclosed by a moat and an entrance pavilion guarded with two stone lions. From there, a steep stairway led up 14 meters and six levels. The first of the five levels incorporated twelve shrines, while the upper-most consisted of a central shrine and four secondary ones. The exact number of shrines and levels served a specific purpose for Yaśovarman's rule. Including the base of the structure, there were seven levels in total, meant to represent the seven levels of heaven. There were also 108 towers that, when divided by four, were meant to symbolize lunar cycle phases. The astronomical observations included the twelve-year cycle of Jupiter through the twelve shrines on five of the levels (Zéphir 1998: 46-47). The importance of the monument was great enough that, despite the possible conflict between Indravarman I and Yaśovarman, Yasódharapura was connected by a causeway to the earlier capital of Hariharālaya.

Yaśovarman died in 910—perhaps due to leprosy, as he was known as the "Leper King"—and was succeeded by his son Harshavarman I (reigned 910-923). Little is known regarding his rule, though it is thought to be a time of political instability. During times of conflict or internal struggle, the construction of monuments—which frequently held inscriptions detailing events of the time—are rare, resulting in a "dark period" of history. It is possible Harshavarman I's maternal uncle, Jayavarman IV, competed for power throughout the king's entire reign. Jayavarman IV lost this struggle for power and was driven away around 921. After that, the reign of Ishanavarman II lasted from 923-928.

During Ishanavarman II's short reign, the king may have been restricted to ruling over the region of Angkor and forced to compete with his uncle, Jayavarman IV, who had been driven out earlier. Jayavarman IV set up a rival capital, 100 kilometers northeast of Angkor. Other than a temple, Prasat Kravan, Ishanavarman II did not order monuments or temples built. Upon his death, the throne was passed on to his rival uncle, Jayavarman IV (reigned 928 to 941), who had a valid claim to the throne through his maternal line.

When Jayavarman IV was exiled in 921, he built Chok Gargyar as his capital (the modern name for the ruins is Koh Ker), a walled city approximately 1,200 square meters surrounded by scattered temples over a 35 square kilometer area. During Jayavarman IV's time there, he built the complexes expected of any ruling king, constructing the Prasat Thom complex, featuring a 30 meter high, seven-level pyramid that likely featured a five-meter high metal linga. The building projects suggest Jayavarman IV saw himself as the rightful ruler to the throne before 928, and the inscriptions back this up, stating that his achievements far surpassed those of previous kings.

In order for Chok Gargyar to have been built over such a short period, the empire would have required a significant amount of administrative control. This means taxes would have been collected and distributed in a controlled fashion, and labor would have to be organized to construct the temples. Despite the successful construction of this new capital, the city would be left to decay over the next thousand years, shortly following Jayavarman IV's death in 941. In 941, Harshavarman II, the son of Jayavarman IV, took the throne for a brief time before he was removed by his cousin, Rajendravarman II, in 944. Rajendravarman II, who ruled until 968, moved the capital back to Yasódharapura.

Inscriptions found on the Pre Rup monument in the Angkor region claim that Rajendravarman II was fierce in combat, and that he had a sword that was constantly soaked in his enemies' blood and was as hard as a diamond. This may be related to Rajendravarman II's acquisition of power, but it may also simply be the king making himself seem larger than life to his people. The king did lead a series of campaigns against the neighboring Champa Empire. Rajendravarman II also claimed to have a royal lineage dating back to the pre-Khmer, Chenla Empire. During his reign, Rajendravarman II brought about more central control over the outlying provinces, largely ruled by local princes, and began construction of Banteay Srei from pink sandstone in Angkor. The ten-year-old son of Rajendravarman II, Jayavarman V (reigned 968 to 1001), succeeded his father.

Since the king was so young, the court officials were largely in control of the politics while Jayavarman V studied Buddhism, medicine, and astronomy under Yajnavaraha (a grandson of Harshavarman I). The temple of Banteay Srei contains a foundation stela claiming Yajnavaraha was one who helped the weak, sick, or those in poverty. Due to these dedications, the temple is believed to have been completed with Yajnavaraha's financial assistance. When the young king turned seventeen-years-old, he began construction on temples of his own, most notably the state temple of Ta Keo. Construction at this temple quickly halted, however, when a bolt of lightning struck it. This was taken as a bad omen, and the state shrine was left unfinished. Despite the king's coming of age, it is likely the court officials still had considerable influence over events. More than the reign of any other Khmer monarch are the ministers, scholars and other dignitaries mentioned in the inscriptions (Briggs 1951: 135). One of the most notable royal families that seemed to have considerable influence during this period was the Saptadevakula family.

During Jayavarman V's reign, Buddhism began to flourish even though the king himself was a Shaivite. Specifically, Mahayana Buddhism began to spread, and the king is said to have imported Buddhists texts to his lands although none of these texts have survived.

Jayavarman V was briefly succeeded by Udayadityavarman I (reigned 1001-1002), who was usurped by Suryavarman I (reigned 1002-1049). In 1002, Suryavarman I challenged

Udayadityavarman I's armies and won, though others claimed the throne. Following Udayadityavarman I's removal, Suryavarman I and Jayaviravarman battled for the throne. The legitimacy of Suryavarman I's claim to the throne is obscure, though he may have had ancestral ties to Malaysia (Higham 1991: 334). It has also been suggested that Suryavarman I was a member of the Saptadevakula lineage, the same family that wielded so much influence during Jayavarman V's reign. The Saptadevakula family claimed lineage to the throne through a connection to Indravarman I, and it is possible this connection helped Suryavarman I ascend to the throne. After 1005, no more is written of Jayaviravarman, and Suryavarman I had settled in Angkor.

The king then began to consolidate his power by making officials pledge their lives to him in sacred ceremonies. He also began to erect lingams were named after him (Suryavarmesvara) in the corners of his kingdom. Other acts to legitimize his rule were the beginning of numerous building projects in Angkor. He erected his palace just north of the Bakheng.

Jayavarman I was succeeded by Udayadityavarman II (reigned 1050 to 1066), although the relationship of Udayadityavarman II to Jayavarman I is unknown. Based on inscriptions from this period, it is clear there were numerous rebellions taking place. His most valuable general during these rebellions was Sangrama. The temple construction he is most known for is the Baphuon Temple in Angkor—devoted to the Hindu god, Shiva—but it also featured Buddhist statues. Harshavarman III (reigned 1066 to 1080), was Udayadityavarman II's oldest brother, and during his reign, he made Baphuon the center of his capital. Like his brother's reign, Harshavarman III's rule was plagued by rebellions. Unlike his brother, Harshavarman III was not able to defeat all of the rebellions, and he was ultimately usurped by Jayavarman VI (reigned 1080 to 1107), who may have come to power through the frequent conflicts Harshavarman III had with neighboring Champa.

Unlike previous rulers, Jayavarman VI did not attempt to trace his lineage back to earlier rulers of Angkor or Chenla. Instead, Jayavarman VI traced his lineage to mythical roots, claiming to have been a descendant of Prince Sage Kambu Swayambhuva and Mera. It is believed he came from the Phimai area of modern day Thailand. He established a new dynasty, the Mahidharapura, and it is likely that early in his reign, he was fraught with conflict from other claimants to the throne. Nevertheless, he was succeeded by his older brother, Dharanindravarman I (reigned 1107 to 1113), who married the wife of his deceased brother and was ultimately murdered by his great-nephew, Sūryavarman II (reigned 1113 to 1145-1150).

Sūryavarman II is best known for the icon structure of Angkor Wat, one of the largest religious structures in the world. Even though he was able to organize the construction of such a monumental building project, his reign was not without conflict with neighboring empires (Higham 2001: 113). In particular, Sūryavarman II struggled with the Đại Việt and Champa empires to the east, while successfully expanding his kingdom further west into modern day Thailand.

While the extravagant galleries at Angkor Wat testify to Sūryavarman II's military prowess, historical records by the Cham detail a much different account of Khmer expeditions against the Đại Việt. These records can be accepted as truth since the Champa state would lend forces to the Khmer military during some of these campaigns. Jaya Indravarman III of the Cham must have seen the futility of these attacks, as he eventually made peace with the Đại Việt, meaning there would be no more assisted attacks for the Khmer. In total, the Cham recorded three failed campaigns against the Đại Việt. The newly-formed peace between the Đại Việt and Champa may have upset Sūryavarman II so much that he ordered the invasion of Champa around 1145. It was an attack that would prove more successful than the ones against the Đại Việt, and the Champa king was removed and replaced with Harideva, a distant relation to Sūryavarman II. The reign of this replacement king was cut short by a retaliation from Champa, and Harideva was swiftly executed, which may have led to further retaliation by the Khmer Empire between 1145 and 1150.

This act of retribution would be the final campaign led by Sūryavarman II and would prove to be his downfall. Although the circumstances or the exact whereabouts of his demise are unknown, it is believed that he died during the offensive against Champa, whether in battle or under other circumstances. Further complicating the circumstances of his death is the fact that his body never made it back to Angkor Wat, his monumental mausoleum.

Angkor Wat was dedicated to Hindu god Vishnu which is unusual since the previous rulers had mainly been devoted to Shiva. The original name of the site is unknown, despite it being the largest religious edifice known (Higham 1991: 19). Continuing building traditions beginning generations before, the complex at Angkor Wat was built with a surrounding 200-meter moat and large megalithic blocks. Within the moat, another wall with four entrances had been erected. This construction largely separated the temple complex from the jungle which helped preserve the ruins for the next thousand years. The temple itself is made up of three walled galleries detailing mythical events and achievements of the king. They also contain the longest continuous reliefs that have ever been carved (ibid). In the so-called historical gallery, the outer-most gallery on the western half of the southern gallery, the king is given his posthumous name, Paramavishnouloka. What this inscription suggests is that Sūryavarman II never lived to see the Angkor Wat finished. The king is depicted—alive and with his posthumous name—elaborately decorated with fine jewelry and heavy body ornaments on his ears, arms, and legs.

Angkor Wat

**Late 19<sup>th</sup> century drawings of Angkor Wat**

In general, Angkor Wat is a three-tiered pyramid with each level or terrace being bounded by galleries and a gopuram for each of the cardinal directions. The upper-most terrace is square, while the two lower terraces are more rectangular, stretching out towards the west. This elongation provided space on the 2nd level for two small "libraries" to be included, while a cloister was included on the first level that connects the galleries along with two much larger "libraries." To understand the import role that Angkor Wat played in Khmer culture, a much more detailed examination of the elements that make up Angkor Wat are needed.

Before even coming close to the temple, a visitor first encounters the moat, which surrounds the external, or fourth enclosure from the center. The moat of Angkor Wat is bounded by megalithic blocks for ten kilometers, while a wall 4.5 meters high encloses the complex itself. Access to Angkor Wat is possible by four entrances, each of which is facing a cardinal direction. The largest of these entrances is on the western side and acts as the central doorway that is accessed by massive sandstone blocks forming a bridge over the moat. Linking the entranceway with the bridge is a cruciform causeway, which was added later, flanked by nāgas (sacred snakes). The mythical serpents, nāgas, are a frequent motif found in Khmer architecture. Similar nāga-bridges can also be found at the nearby Angkor Thom. The nāga is typically depicted with multiple heads that are uneven in number and spread apart, forming a fan-like projection similar to that of a cobra. The nāgas were symbolic to the Khmer for water, but also were a major part of the Khmer origin mythology. One myth traces the origins of the Khmer people to the coupling of a Brahman and a nāga princess of Cambodia. The causeway continues inside leading to the three galleries and central tower. Once inside the main entrance, there are two small "libraries" and water basins on either side.

The main western entrance consists of a gopuram, or pavilion, and five entryways. The use of a gopuram is borrowed from Indian architecture in which a monumental tower would be made as an entrance to a temple. This style of architecture was being used and elaborated upon in India during the same time Angkor Wat was being constructed. However, in the 12th century, the Pandya rulers of India had begun making the gopura so elaborate that they overshadowed the central temple itself. The gopura of Angkor Wat and other temples in Angkor, while elaborate and impressive, do not overshadow the central temples.

The gopuram consists of three porticos with elephant gates to the north and south. It is unknown how much the general Khmer public would have been able to see of this temple or if they were allowed even through the western gopuram, however it seems likely that the privileged and royal elite would have been active here. The gopuram is crowned with three towers that have since fallen into decay. In its heyday, the gopuram would have blocked the view of visitors as they approached, yet the silhouette of the gopuram itself would mimic the view of the actual monument. This minor addition keeps the focus on the monument itself and the theme that Sūryavarman II wished to present. In a way, minor additions such as this and others to come were a way for Sūryavarman II to control every aspect of the experience that the visitor had when they visited his celestial mountain on earth.

The western-facing direction itself is significant. It is linked with the setting of the sun and therefore also commonly associated with death. This would make sense for the mausoleum of Sūryavarman II to be facing the west. Vishnu, who is also commonly featured on the temple, is also often associated with the west. However, temples oriented to the west and dedicated to divinities are uncommon, making Angkor Wat unique. Of course, while the temple itself opens to the west, the visitor would be forced to look east as they approached. This also meant the visitor would be moving towards the rising of the sun, which is associated with new life.

As the visitor would pass through the gopuram, they would proceed up steps, beginning the symbolic journey up the sacred mountain. The causeway itself would have been an impressive sight and indeed remains a famed tourist attraction today. The visitor would have had their view of the temple blocked by the towers of the western gopuram and then would have had to pass through the natural darkness the gopuram created. As they came through to the opposite side, their eyes would have had to adjust to the light, especially if the sun was rising over the temple from the east. The effect of such a sight would have given one the feeling of entering a sacred realm. Before the visitor would lie the 350-meter by about 8-meter causeway built on a raised earth fill. The raised walkway was paved with sandstone and flanked by mythical nagas that were designed to be visually stunning, with a mixture of sunlight and shadow. Along the walkway on the north and south sides are six breaks for staircases that are marked with elaborate nāga heads.

The fourth set of stairs on either side leads down to the first set of libraries. These likely would have been more accessible to the lower class of visitor, given their relation to the main temple. Stylistically, these libraries are lower to the ground and feature four large porticoes with large pillars. Ten large open windows on the north and south sides allow a significant amount of light inside as well as adequate air flow. This open and light style of design may have allowed these libraries to act as gathering places for larger groups of people than would be possible in the other libraries. These libraries are relatively common features of Khmer temple architecture, although their exact function is not known. It is likely that they served broader religious functions, rather than as exclusive repositories of manuscripts or other texts. These freestanding buildings would be frequently found in pairs with openings to the west, however, the pair found on the lowest terrace of Angkor Wat contain openings to the east and the west. Unfortunately, the significance of this is unknown.

The main causeway crosses the 4th enclosure, and as the visitor walks east toward the central temple, they can look back at the gopuram they have passed through and observe more fine details of the western entrance. Facing east on the eastern exterior of the western gopuram are apsaras or devatas (divine female spirits) that are carved in groups of two to three or occasionally individually. These apsaras are depicted as beautiful supernatural beings that are meant to be at the service of a god. Symbolically, they are forever facing the east, which is linked to the rising of the sun and to the concept of new life. This is likely a reference to Sūryavarman II who was strongly associated with the sun. The style of these apsaras is significant, as they each feature unique hairstyles and jewelry that perhaps reflected actual styles of dress of the time.

As the visitor continues down the causeway, the visitor would ascend a cruciform terrace which would lead to the main entrance and the 3rd enclosure. Flanking the stairways to this terrace are groups of lions looking westward towards the approaching visitor. As the visitor ascends these gradual steps -- the symbolic climb up the mountain -- they can view the main entrance that appears similar to the western gopuram with the central temple and two smaller temples dominating the view. Of course, these are the actual temples and destination and not an aesthetic, as in the western gopuram. It is likely that on such a large raised terrace in front of the symbolic Mount Meru, rituals and dances were held. The surrounding land of the 4th enclosure and the ability for elephants and large parades to pass through the Western gopuram would have allowed a significant number of people to attend ceremonies here.

Without having to even enter the 3rd enclosure through the entrance on the raised terrace, people would have been able to walk around and view the gallery enclosing the 3rd terrace. The galleries surrounding Angkor Wat are important in understanding the role Angkor Wat played in Khmer culture, since these scenes were so significant that they were meant to be viewed on the outside of the central sanctuary. The 3rd gallery, which is the outermost one that encloses the lowest terrace and the one the visitor would encounter first, features a series of images and scenes divided up into the north, south, east, and west galleries, with each of these galleries being divided in half. The galleries depict not only royal life and events, but also display epic scenes from the Hindu epic poem, the Ramayana. Standing on the large raised terrace in front of the main entrance, to the left of the visitor facing east would be the northern part of the western gallery, and to their right would be the southern part of the western gallery.

The gallery itself is approximately 187 meters by 215 meters with a two-and-a-half-meter wide vaulted walkway that featured double aisles with the columns being on the outside of the inner aisle and on either side for the outer aisle. On the exterior of the wall are bas-reliefs two meters high and covering around 1,000 square meters in total. The scenes depicted were cut directly into the surface of the wall and thanks to the vaulted double aisle covering have suffered only minimal damage over the hundreds of years since their creation. From these carvings, different styles can be seen which is likely due to the use of different artisans for different sections of the gallery. It is likely that the gallery was meant to be viewed in a counterclockwise fashion, based on funerary rights of *prasavya*, which is Sanskrit for anti-clockwise (Bronkhorst 2011: 214), from the terraced main entrance -- that is to say, beginning in the southern part of the western gallery.

Beginning with the southern half of the western gallery, which would be located on the righthand side of the visitor at the main entrance, is a single panel composition depicting a scene from the Mahabharata, a major Hindu epic. This scene is of the battle of Kurukshetra and contains the four divisions of the Mahabharata. From the northern section of the panel, the Kauravas are approaching the Pandavas. The scene depicts the typical hierarchy that can be found in the other panels with the lower-class infantry on the bottom, the officers and elephant riders on the next tier, and the commanders on the upper 3rd tier. Kurukshetra means "field of Kurus" and refers to the battlefield in which two rival clans within the Kuru family fought. This was an important battle in the Hindu epic, making up a significant portion of the Mahabharata, even though it lasted only eighteen days.

The western half of the southern gallery, also known as the "historical gallery," depicts a royal audience and court session with the king being depicted as larger than life. The entire ninety-meter panel is devoted to the builder of Angkor Wat, Sūryavarman II. Historically, this is a significant depiction as it is the first time in Angkorian history that such a depiction has been made. The king is given his posthumous name, Paramavishnouloka, suggesting that this panel or inscription was made after the death of the king. He is elaborately decorated with fine jewelry and heavy body ornaments for the ears, arms and legs. He is seated on a throne with fourteen parasols as he meets with his ministers. He also holds a dead snake in his right hand and an unidentified object in his left. The gallery continues with a depiction of a mountain side and a progression making its way down. In the progression is the king riding an elephant. Accompanying the king are the *rajahotar* (royal priests) and generals who also ride elephants.

The chiefs are ranked according to the number of parasols that they have with them and small inscriptions beside them. The panel also depicts different contingents of troops that the king is inspecting during the parade. This is also significant since some troops are depicted as bare chested and barefoot, while others are shown with specific styles of hair dress and weaponry that is not typical of the Khmer. This suggests that the Khmer army was a coalition that incorporated forces from outside the local region or from other mandalas. One such army was the Lavo army that is depicted with the same characteristics as the Khmer army. This Lavo force was led by Sri Jaya Simhavarman. Interestingly, he is depicted with seventeen parasols, or three more than the King even. The most any of the other generals or chiefs have are twelve parasols. Lavo, also known as Lavodayapura in the Khmer language, was a subordinate mandala of the Khmer empire that became more independent by the end of the 13th century. The capital of this mandala was in modern-day Lopburi, Thailand, where Angkorian-style architecture can still be found.

Other troops wear distinctive helmets featuring deer-heads. The military style parade eventually transitions into a ritual parade with *Radzhahotara* (royal sacrificial priests) and the Siamese who were allies with the Khmer at the time.

The eastern half of the southern gallery depicts the judgment of the dead by Yama, the god of the dead. This scene essentially depicts heaven (or paradise) and hell. Inscriptions in this gallery reveal that there are thirty-two levels of hell and thirty-seven levels of heaven. Royals, or well-to-do people, are shown as ascending into heaven, while the less fortunate or poor are beginning their journey into hell. While the scenes of heaven depict the offering of gifts by women in celestial palaces, the scenes of hell are much more elaborate and detailed. Heaven is held up by garduas and lions, while scenes of the crucifixion of thieves via nails to the head (as a punishment for stealing flowers from the garden of Shiva) are depicted below. The twenty-3rd circle of hell depicts a variety of sinners being roasted over fire, and the 10th circle depicts the bones of sinners being broken as punishment for damaging property. One special occurrence in heaven is the possible depiction of Suryavarman II in paradise.

Although the scenes of torture and punishment are explicit, they were not viewed as eternal damnation, but rather as transitionary phases that the person would pass through. The Hindu religion did not believe in eternal damnation, and even the torturers or executioners were also being punished.

The southern half of the east gallery depicts another famous scene from Hindu mythology: the *samudra manthana*, or the churning of the ocean (or sea of milk). This scene can be found in the Mahabharata (Ganguli 1883: Section XVIII), the Vishnu Purana (Wilson 1840: Chapter IX), as well as the Ramayana (Griffith 1870: Canto XLV). The scene depicts the Asuras, or demons, totaling ninety-two, and Devas, totaling eighty-eight, working together to churn the ocean to create the nectar of immortality. Used as a churning rod is Mount Mandara with the king of the serpents, Vasuki, being used as the churning rope. The demons are depicted as holding the head portion of the snake, while the Devas hold the tail portion. The outcome of the churning of the ocean, also known as the ocean of milk, was to be the nectar of immortality, known as *Amrita,* that the Devas and demons would share. Vishnu, however, arranged that the Devas alone would be the ones who drank the nectar. After a battle for the nectar ensues, the Devas overcome the demons with the help of Vishnu and Garuda. According to the story, this entire process took a thousand years to be accomplished.

The northern half of the east gallery is similar in style and theme features Vishnu's victory over the asuras. This section was added later than the original construction, sometime between the 16th and 18th century. Vishnu stands in the middle of the gallery and is being converged upon from both sides by the Asura. Vishnu is depicted with four arms and sitting on the shoulders of Garuda. He has wreaked havoc over the rival armies and sent them fleeing. One group is mounted on gigantic birds, although the significance of this is lost.

The eastern part of the north gallery depicts Krishna's victory over the Asura, Bana. Krishna appears with eight arms and riding Garuda, his mount, on multiple occasions in the scene. In one part of the scene, the god of fire, Agni, rides a rhinoceros and has deployed a wall of fire that

Garuda must face. In another, a Garuda-riding Krishna appears fighting a multi-armed Bana who is pulled in a chariot by lion-like monsters. Krishna manages to severe all but two of Bana's thousand hands and is victorious. Krishna is seen kneeling at Mount Kailasa at the feet of Shiva where he agreed to spare Bana's life. This panel is an example of lesser craftsmanship in its execution.

Continuing around the 3rd outer most gallery counterclockwise, the next gallery (the western part of the north gallery), features another combat scene of an unspecified battle between the Devas, or gods, and the Asuras. This infinite battle takes place over Heaven, Earth and the Nether world between two races with strong religious powers. The history of these two races is long in Hinduism, however, in general this can be seen as a battle between good and evil with the Devas being the good and the Asuras being the bad.

The battle itself features a series of duels with twenty-one identifiable gods struggling with a similar Asura. These gods are recognizable by what they are carrying in their hands and by their mounts, although their Asura adversary is almost identical, save for the different hairstyle. Here, the craftsmanship is obviously of a higher quality than the previous gallery.

The northern part of the western gallery depicts scenes from the Ramayana, specifically the climactic Battle of Lanka in which Rama rides on the shoulders of the monkey-king, Hanuman. Visually, the scene is an epic entanglement of monkeys and *rakshasas* (man-eaters) (Maurice 1944). According to the Ramayana, Hanuman, the monkey commander of Rama's army, fought with Rama against Ravana, King of Lanka, in order to retrieve Rama's wife, Sita. In a single leap, Hanuman jumped from India to Lanka in search of Sita. When he was discovered, his tail was set on fire, which he then used to burn down Lanka. From there, Hanuman flew to the Himalayas to bring back medicine for the wounded in Rama's army. Like the other heroes of the Ramayana, Hanuman's steadfast and pure character traits are to be admired. As a deity, he is worshipped in numerous temples dedicated to Rama and in some cases in temples devoted to him exclusively. While Hanuman is a popular deity in southern India, he is also worshipped in Tibet. Rama and Hanuman, along with his army of monkeys, battle the ten-headed demon-king, Ravana, who is equipped with twenty arms for the freedom of Rama's kidnapped wife, Sita. As the story goes, the demon king is eventually defeated, and Rama returns to Ayodhya to become king (Ricci 2014).

The gallery may have been as close as some of the common visitors were able to get to the central temple, while more aristocratic or elite visitors were allowed inside. Proceeding up the steps of the terrace, the visitor enters the 3rd enclosure and the first level of the temple pyramid. The 3rd enclosure features a library to the north and south, while between these two structures is the gallery, known today as the Cruciform Cloister. This cloister, which links the 3rd and the 2nd enclosures together, features two pools. Later, when the temple became a site of Buddhism, this western portion of the cloister would come to be known as the Gallery of a Thousand Buddhas.

The eastern half of the gallery has become known as the Chamber of Echoes. Surrounding the entire cloister are apsaras in the frieze.

The theme of apsaras overlooking the sacred mountain continues on the 2nd level (also the 2nd enclosure). The gallery of the 2nd level is surrounded by another walled gallery featuring approximately 1,500 apsaras. Like the other apsaras of the western gopuram, these also each feature unique hairstyles and jewelry.

The final level would have been restricted to the high priests and select royals. The final ascension would have led to a statue of Vishnu and would have represented the end of the symbolic journey up the sacred mountain.

Other symbolic aspects of Angkor Wat would not have been entirely visual for the visitor. For example, the lowest common denominator in Khmer, *hat,* measuring roughly .435 meters, was used symbolically in the construction. The length and width of the main structure in the center was 365.37 *hat,* and the distance of the four causeways represented the great eras in the Hindu conception of time. The structure was also influenced by the lunar cycles and acted as a calendar in stone that could predict lunar eclipses. Furthermore, on the spring equinox a visitor on the western entrance could view the sunrise directly over the central tower. This was likely meant to be a reference to Sūryavarman II, which means "Sun King."

The temple was built using a combination of sandstone, known as *thma puok*, and brick. The sandstone of Angkor likely came from a large quarry approximately forty kilometers away. Transportation from the quarry to Angkor would have been done by a combination of water transport, being carried by hand, and pulled on rollers. Evidence of lifting or moving techniques can be found on the stones in forms of holes. These regularly spaced holes would have been used to place wooden pegs that could then be attached to ropes or as clasp holders for hoists. These would have allowed the stones to be maneuvered more precisely and easily into place during construction. After the stones were in place, the holes were filled, either with fitted stones or with mortar plugs.

### The Decline of the Khmer Empire

Around the time of Angkor Wat's construction, the Khmer Empire was at the height of its power. Surrounding the Khmer Empire were the Champa state, located in the south of modern Vietnam, the Đại Việt in the north of modern Vietnam, Mon kingdoms in Myanmar, and other kingdoms of the Malay Peninsula. Expansion into these territories often came with force, although there were also times of peace.

In times of war, the Khmer typically used a variety of ranged weapons. Based on bas-reliefs and other archaeological data, historians know the Khmer army was well-organized and divided into infantry, cavalry, the charioteers, and soldiers on elephants. The divisions of troops relying upon horses were deemed impractical since the horses were not native to Southeast Asia and therefore needed to be imported at great expense. The ground troops had a number of ranged weapons at their disposal, such as spears, bows and arrows, and perhaps a type of catapult for shooting arrows. These larger catapults, according to engravings, were attached to elephants when taken into battle.

**Gisling's picture of a Khmer engraving that depicts archers on elephants**

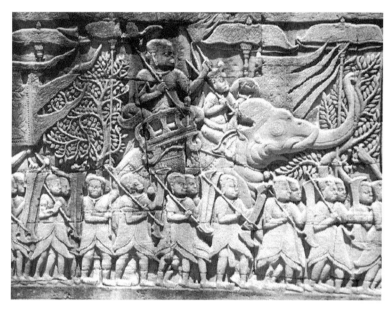

**Manfred Werner's picture of a Khmer engraving that depicts the army**

The proximity of Angkor to sources of water also meant the Khmer had to develop a formidable naval force to prevent attackers that could successfully navigate the difficult Mekong River. It also provided the Khmer with an ideal route on which to attack regions in the north and, if needed, the south. The Khmer navy featured long boats, approximately 20 meters in length, propelled by oars. Carvings from the Bayon display scenes of naval battles against Cham forces.

**Mark Alexander's picture of an engraving depicting naval warfare against the Cham**

While the architecture and art of the Khmer Empire was at its height during the construction of Angkor Wat, the empire quickly declined after Sūryavarman II's death, with a number of usurper rulers competing for the throne (Maurice 1944). At first, Sūryavarman II was succeeded by his cousin, Dharanindravarman II (reigned 1150 to 1160), who had a son, Jayavarman VII, with the daughter of Harshavarman III. Little is known of his rule, and he was succeeded by Yasovarman II (reigned 1160 to 1165), who was, in turn, assassinated by Tribhuvanadityavarman (reigned 1165 to 1177), a mandarin who then proclaimed himself king.

**A bust depicting Jayavarman VII**

The rule of this mandarin king was brought to an end by a usurper king in Champa. In 1177, King Jaya Indravarman IV of the Cham led a successful surprise attack on the Angkor Empire, resulting in the looting of Angkor Wat and Tribhuvanadityavarman's execution. The waterways that had allowed early pre-Khmer mandalas to prosper through trade with India and China were key to Jaya Indravarman IV's attack. When the king could not procure sufficient horses from China to mount a land assault, he amassed a large naval fleet instead, with which to sail up the Mekong to attack the Tonlé Sap.

The invading Cham forces were eventually driven out by Jayavarman VII (reigned 1181 to 1219) in 1178. After restoring order to the capital and ending conflicts between smaller, warring factions within the Khmer Empire, he crowned himself king in 1181 (Higham 2001). After establishing control over his empire, Jayavarman VII attacked Champa in 1191 and made it part of the Khmer Empire. In addition to regaining control over the Khmer Empire and providing stabilization, he was also a devoted Mahayana Buddhist who built numerous constructions for his people. It is likely these projects were meant to help alleviate the suffering of the people since Jayavarman VII saw himself as a Buddha (Coedes 1968: 147). The constructions included rest houses along far-stretching roads and hospitals. He also built numerous military constructions during his reign, more than any previous ruler had ever done. This is perhaps in response to the chaotic nature under which he obtained the throne. Ironically, the numerous building projects meant to help the people and protect them also placed significant drain and stress on economic and natural resources for the Khmer Empire.

One of Jayavarman VII's most notable constructions is Jayagiri, meaning "Victory Mountain." The modern name for the temple is Bayon, given to it by the French due to the Buddhist imagery, and the Banyan tree, which is of particular significance in Buddhism. The temple was constructed 1.7 kilometers north of Angkor Wat, in the Angkor Thom complex, in the center of the new capital of Indrapattha. Despite the French bestowing a Buddhist-related name on the temple, there are actually numerous Hindu elements incorporated into the architecture. The galleries of the Bayon are overwhelmingly devoted to military expeditions, such as naval battles against the Cham. They also offer insight into everyday life and provide a rare glimpse at housing construction, which is difficult to uncover archaeologically. At the center of the temple, a giant, 3.6 meter-high statue of Jayavarman VII as the Buddha king is featured sitting beneath the coils of a naga.

**Mark Alexander's picture of a Khmer engraving on Bayon that depicts a market**

Jayavarman VII died in 1219 and was succeeded by Indravarman II (reigned 1219 to 1243). There is very little known about the reign of this king, and this is likely on purpose. Following Indravarman II's death, Jayavarman VIII (reigned 1243 to 1295) took control of the empire and went about making Hinduism the official religion of the Khmer Empire. This was in contrast to the Buddhist works of the previous two kings, and it is possible Jayavarman VIII went about destroying records and inscriptions of Indravarman II's deeds. What is known about the Khmer Empire during Indravarman II's reign can be inferred from the historical records of other kingdoms. The Khmer Empire had begun to lose control of some of its territories. The Champa took territories from the east, and the emerging Sukhothai Kingdom also began taking some of the western lands. Sukhothai's secession from the Khmer Empire around 1238 may have begun much earlier, in 1180. The founding of the Sukhothai Kingdom would later be considered the beginning of the history of modern-day Thailand for the Thai people.

The peaceful reign and the loss of lands under Indravarman II seems to have been a sign of weakness and opportunity for enemy forces, leaving Jayavarman VIII to endure multiple attacks from outside forces, mainly Mongol forces led by Kublai Khan which began attacking the Khmer Empire in 1283, and may have also been the result of Jayavarman VIII imprisoning Mongol emissaries in 1281. Perhaps unable to withstand the onslaught of Mongol forces, Jayavarman VIII decided to pay tribute to obtain peace with the Mongols, which was overshadowed by the conflict with the Sukhothai Kingdom. Jayavarman VIII had been struggling with them and had little success. These conflicts may have led Jayavarman VIII to abdicate or be overthrown in 1295 by Indravarman III (reigned 1295 to 1308), the brother-in-law of Jayavarman VIII and a Buddhist. In an attempt to undo what Jayavarman VIII had done with Hinduism, Indravarman III attempted to make Buddhism the state religion of the Khmer people, though he practiced Theravada Buddhism as opposed to the Mahayana Buddhism of his predecessors. Theravada Buddhism is based on the Pali Canon and written in the Pali language. In practice, Theravada Buddhism tends to be more conservative in terms of doctrine, and this form of Buddhism is still a major religion of Southeast Asia today.

During this time, Chinese diplomats had visited the Khmer Empire and documented what they had seen. The most famous of these accounts was written by Zhou Daguan and titled *The Customs of Cambodia*. According to Daguan, the people did not wear tops or anything on their feet, whether male or female. "From the king down, the men and women all wear hair wound up in a knot, and go naked to the waist, wrapped only in a cloth. When they are not out and about, they wind a larger piece of cloth over the small one. Only the king can wear material with a full pattern of flowers on it. On his head he wears a gold crown…Sometimes he goes without a crown, and simply wears a chain of fragrant flowers such as jasmine wound round the braids of hair. Around his neck he wears a large pearl weighing about four pounds (two kilograms). On his wrists and ankles and all his fingers and toes he wears gold bracelets and rings." (Daguan 1297: 50)

Daguan also details the diets of the Khmer people, and what he wrote matches what is shown in temple carvings. The commoners had a diet consisting largely of rice and fish, while the more well-to-do had fruits and vegetables in their diets. It is known from carvings that royals, such as the king, would be served meats such as pig, but the carvings do not provide many details regarding how commoners lived and ate. Daguan was able to provide valuable insight, writing, "Ordinary families have houses but nothing else by way of tables, chairs, jars, or buckets. They use a clay pot to cook rice in, and make sauce with a clay saucepan. For a stove they sink three stones in the ground, and for spoons they use coconut husks…When serving rice they use clay or copper dishes from China; sauce comes in a small bowl made from the leaves of a tree, which

does not leak even when filled with liquid. They also make small spoons from the leaves of the nypa palm, which they spoon liquid into their mouths with, and throw away after using."
(Daguan 1297: 76)

Historical sources such as these are significant, since around this period, there seems to have been an archaeological "dark age." It is known that following Indravarman III's rule, Indrajayavarman reigned (1308 to 1327), followed by Jayavarman IX (reigned 1327 to 1336). Jayavarman IX, the son of Indrajayavarman III, was assassinated, and he is the last king to be mentioned in Sanskrit on monuments.

Further historical knowledge of this period comes from other kingdoms, such as the newly-formed Kingdom of Ayutthaya, which emerged by conquering the Sukhothai Kingdom in the north before turning on the Khmer Empire to the east. The frequent conflicts taking place in Angkor at this time had weakened the presence of the Khmer in the Chao Phraya River Plain, allowing Ayutthaya to easily take control.

Ayutthaya's assaults were generally successful, if short-lived. Typically, a Siamese prince was placed on the throne to rule, but he would be quickly assassinated or driven out. So successful and prevalent were these attacks that in 1431, King Ponhea Yat (reigned 1405 to 1463) moved the Khmer Empire center from Angkor to Phnom Penh. This move marked the official end of the Khmer Empire.

In addition to external forces causing the decline of the Khmer Empire, environmental factors also likely contributed. As discussed above, the waters of the Tonlé Sap and the Mekong provided the people with food, water for irrigation and drinking, trade, travel, and communication with partners. The development of large-scale construction projects, such as those at Angkor, required large-scale clearing of the forests while the larger populations required more food, also requiring significant forest-clearing for rice fields. This may have had a significant effect on the water systems on which they depended. Without the roots of the forest trees to hold the soil together, water runoff after the rains brings a significant amount of soil. The irrigation canal routes would not have been able to handle such excessive amounts of soil run-off and could easily have become clogged over time. This, in turn, would kill fish and crops due to the lack of flowing water.

Without an excess of food for trade, the Khmer Empire's economy suffered. In such a scenario, even short periods of drought would be catastrophic for the people. These environmental factors, when coupled with Jayavarman VII's extensive building projects and the resources needed to maintain a large, standing army to protect the vast empire would have put a significant amount of strain on the empire as a whole, thus bringing about its decline. There is also the possibility, although it has yet to be backed-up with archaeological evidence, that the bubonic plague, which is known to have been in China around 1345, may have spread down the Mekong River to affect the Khmer Empire.

The memory of the Khmer Empire has never really been forgotten or lost, despite what early European visitors thought in the age of colonialism (Ricci 2015). In fact, attempts to bring the central court back to Angkor were made during the 16th century, and although they failed, there is evidence Angkor continued to be inhabited from 1431 onward. In the 20th century, Angkor yet again became a site of pilgrimage, and millions of tourists now flock there annually. Angkor Wat, in particular, has become a cultural icon of Cambodia, and the tourism generated by Angkor itself provides 28.3% of the country's gross domestic product (Turner 2016), making it one of the nation's largest industries.

Tourism and the protection of the Khmer Empire's archaeological sites ensure the history and memory of this empire will not be lost to future generations.

**Pictures of Angkor Wat**

**Entrance to Banteay Srei moat and causeway.**

Banteay Srei courtyard.

Remains of Shiva shrines Banteay Srei  square openings once held phallic symbols the square is symbolic of Vishnu, the base of the phallic statue is octagonal representing Brahma and the base is the sanadroni, a symbolic vulva.

Banteay Srei inner courtyard.

Banteay Rei central shrine.

**Inner court, Banteay Srei.**

Scene from Ramayana, fire in Khandava forest with Indra above commanding rain to quench flames.

Guardian figures Banteay Rei human in foreground, monkeys in background.

**Gate with Shiva figure.**

**Banteay Srei ativar of Vishu clawing demon.**

**Banteay Srei gate - Lintel with Indra on three headed elephant Airavata.**

**Temple of Phimeanakas.**

**Phimeanakas raised pavilion.**

**Staircase to upper levels of Phimeanakas.**

Phimeanakas East entrance.

**Statues in disarray at base of Phimeanakas**

**Online Resources**

Other books about the Khmer on Amazon

**Further Reading**

Briggs, Lawrence P. 1951. The Ancient Khmer Empire. Transactions of the American Philosophical Society

Coedes, George. 1968. In: Vella, Walter (Ed.) The Indianized States of Southeast Asia. Hawaii: University of Hawaii Press

Cotterell, Arthur and Storm, Rachel. 2009. *The Ultimate Encyclopedia of Mythology*. London: Hermes House

Daguan, Zhou. 1297. *A Record of Cambodia*. Harris, Peter (trans.). 2007. Silkworm Books

Deedrick, Tami. 2002. *Khmer Empire*. Austin, Texas: Raintree Steck-Vaughn

Higham, Charles. 1991. The Archaeology of Mainland Southeast Asia From 10,000 B.C. to the Fall of Angkor. Cambridge University Press: Cambridge.

Higham, Charles. 1996. Khmer Civilization and the Empire of Angkor. p. 370-372. In: Fagan, Brian. 1996. *The Oxford Companion to Archaeology*. Oxford: Oxford University Press

Higham, Charles. 2001. The Civilization of Angkor. London: Weidenfeld & Nicolson

Higham, Charles. 2004. Encyclopedia of Ancient Asian Civilizations. New York: Facts on File, Inc.

Higham, Charles. 2013. *The Origins of the Civilization of Angkor*. London: Bloomsbury

Maurice, Glaize. 1944. *The Monuments of the Angkor Group*.

Ricci, Glenn Arthur. 2014. *Eigen und Fremd in Glaubenswelten*. Oldenburg: Isensee Verlag

Ricci, Glenn Arthur. 2015. *Böser Wilder, friedlicher Wilder. Wie Museen das Bild anderer Kulturen prägen*. Oldenburg: Isensee Verlag

Turner, Rochelle. 2016. *Travel & Tourism Economic Impact 2017 Cambodia*. Word Travel and Tourism Council. (Accessed 01 January 2018: https://www.wttc.org/-/media/files/reports/economic-impact-research/countries-2017/cambodia2017.pdf)

Vickery, Michael 1998. *Society, economics, and politics in pre-Angkor Cambodia: the 7th–8th centuries*. Toyo Bunko

Zéphir, Thierry. 1998. *Khmer, the Lost Empire of Cambodia*. New York: Abrams

## Free Books by Charles River Editors

We have brand new titles available for free most days of the week. To see which of our titles are currently free, <u>click on this link</u>.

## Discounted Books by Charles River Editors

We have titles at a discount price of just 99 cents everyday. To see which of our titles are currently 99 cents, click on this link.

Made in the USA
Middletown, DE
11 September 2020

19477652R00033